PHOENIX SET FREE

WRITTEN BY
MARINA SAMSON

This is a work of fiction. All of the characters, names, incidents, organizations, and dialogue in this novel are either the products of the author's imagination or are used fictitiously.

Archway Publishing books may be ordered through booksellers or by contacting:

Archway Publishing
1663 Liberty Drive
Bloomington, IN 47403
www.archwaypublishing.com
844-669-3957

ESV - One Scripture

ISBN: 978-1-6657-2694-8 (sc)
ISBN: 978-1-6657-2695-5 (e)

Print information available on the last page.

Archway Publishing rev. date: 08/09/2022

Phoenix set free
Rise from the ashes and breath
Coal and brimstone falling down
Emerging a beauty undeniably proud
Wonderful in her glory
The ashes are her life's story From a pile of rubble at dawn
At the darkness of dusk
A phenomenon

Flying through the sky at great heights
Memories of pain ingrained as she takes flight
Soaring over the doom and fury
The hardships she will soon bury
As the phoenix flies towards the sun
The past she so leaves is after her But she faces the mistakes head on
And decides never to run

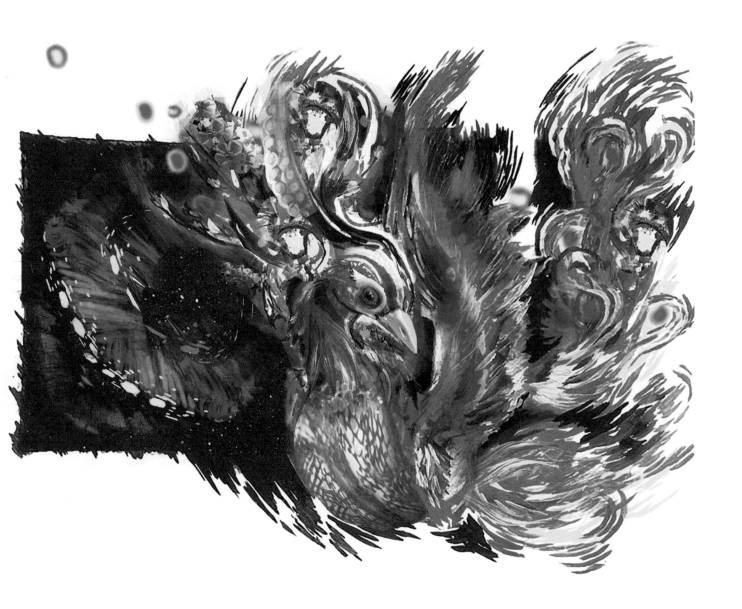

The beautiful phoenix with feathers turquoise, gold and blue
A tail spanning 30 feet with gems of purple and red, remarkable and true
Her eyes, piercing, with a golden-brown hue
And the beak she crowns is a majestic site too
Adorned with striking magenta sparkles
Only the innocent can see her and marvel
Whose eyes are so pure
Blocked out are the bad ones Like an ailment cure
As the phoenix faces her past
She makes peace and conquers at last
Blowing out one single breath A light of diamonds encompasses the dark
The past is transformed into a bright blue lark

That follows the phoenix wherever she may go

A tiny reminder of a battle won by facing her foe

The phoenix and lark become partners for good

Entering the homes of the innocent ones in the woods

Erasing the nightmares of dreams that are scary

They fight together to breath colorful
visions to ones that are weary
New dreams that give the children
hope and comfort
As many of them have homes
that are not triumphant

Until one day they meet an anomaly

A gentle old man humming humbly

In a shack of the woods of the village they visit

The old man looks at the lark and the phoenix

With ocean blue eyes that no one can fix

You see, he was blind, sitting in the chair and rocking

The only company he ever got was the children when
they were selling cookies and knocking

With a toothless grin, the old man could clearly see

The phoenix and lark in the room as brightly can be

Everything else is surrounded in black

The glorious view of magnificence was evident in that shack

With one final breath, the old man just smiled

He turned into a purple cloud twisting furiously and flying wild

Flying across the shack that he lived in

He was entrapped but looked at himself within

The only thing he saw in that fury of purple cloud

Was a brand-new set of magenta eyes
as the phoenix cried out loud

The phoenix and lark looked as happy as can
be, as the phoenix dabbed her eyes

A new set of eyes replaced the honey brown
ones and made her more wise

She finally met the father above
The holy spirit, the lark
The new transformation from ashes
to beauty was Jesus's spark
Her father that gave her eyes to see fully
To see clearly ahead Guided by God
She found her homestead

Printed in the United States
by Baker & Taylor Publisher Services